Twist and Turn

Thirteen Stories with Questions

Gordon Hogg

Illustrations by Shirley Verhoeven

Edward Arnold

©Gordon Hogg 1987

First published in Great Britain 1987
by Edward Arnold (Publishers) Ltd
41 Bedford Square
London WC1B 3DQ

Edward Arnold (Australia) Pty Ltd,
80 Waverley Road
Caulfield East 3145
PO Box 234
Melbourne

British Library Cataloguing in Publication Data
Hogg, Gordon
  Twist and turn: twelve stories with
  questions.
  1. English language—Examinations,
  questions, etc.
  I. Title
  428.2   PE1112
  ISBN 0-7131-7527-3

Text set in 13/17 Century Schoolbook
by Avocet Marketing Services, Bicester, Oxon
Printed by J. W. Arrowsmith Ltd., Bristol
Bound by W. H. Ware and Sons Ltd, Clevedon, Avon

Contents

This is a collection of 13 short, highly illustrated stories designed to stimulate children between 9 and 13 years of age by providing subject matter with which they can identify.

Each story aims to introduce stimulating or amusing reading material, to give practice in basic comprehension and written exercises and to provide further opportunities for 'personal' creative writing, with a cartoon option for a short story and by inviting a piece of longer personal writing.

Pupils can complete activities unaided, but best results will be achieved if discussion precedes written work.

1

The Trick

Joe and Jim were in their classroom. It was lunchtime. They were going to play a trick on Sammy Samson.

'I'm going to get Sammy with this,' Joe said. He had a plastic bag.
'What are you going to do?' asked his pal.
'I'm going to fill it with water,' replied Joe.

He filled the bag with water and took it to the door. Then he stood on a chair. He opened the door a little and placed the bag on top of it. 'Sammy will open the door and the bag will fall on him,' he said.

The two boys sat down to wait. Soon they heard footsteps. Joe ran to the door and looked. Sammy was coming! Joe went back to sit with Jim. The footsteps came closer.
'He's coming!' said Jim.
'Quiet! He'll hear us,' said Joe.

There were more footsteps. Sammy came closer and closer, until he was outside the door. Then he stopped. There was something funny about that door. What was it? There was a drip of water on the floor. He looked up. He saw the water bag, and he knew what to do.

He cried out, 'Hello there, Sir! Please, Sir, can I help you to carry all those books to the room? Right then, Mr King! You go first!'

Inside the room, Joe and Jim jumped up. 'It's King Kong! It's the teacher! He's going to come in!' they cried. 'Quick! Let's get the water bag! Get it down!'

They ran to the door and jumped up to get the water bag. Joe bumped Jim. Jim bumped the door. The door closed. The bag fell.   It landed on Joe's head.

'Aah!' he cried. The water went all over his hair, his face, down his neck and on his clothes. Then he just sat there.

Jim opened the door. No-one was there. 'Where are they?' he said.

Joe got to his feet. He looked out of the door. He looked to the left, and then to the right. There was no-one there. There was no Sammy, and there was no King Kong!

'Oh no!' said Joe.

'What?' asked Jim.

'Sammy tricked us,' replied Joe.

A **Answer these questions in sentences.**

1 What time was it at school?
2 What sort of bag did Joe have?
3 What did he put in it?
4 Where did he put the bag?
5 Why did he do this?
6 Choose the correct ending:
Sammy stopped outside the door because...

a he saw Joe and Jim inside the room.
b there was something odd about the door.

7 Write down the correct sentence:

a Sammy saw the water bag because it was so big.
b Sammy saw the water bag because it had dripped water.

8 Why did Joe and Jim try to take the water bag down from the door?
9 Why did the bag fall on Joe?
10 How did Sammy trick Joe and Jim? Start with these words:
Here is how Sammy tricked the two boys. When he got to the door, he saw...

B **Copy out this puzzle.**

Find these 10 words and put rings round them:

The first one has been done for you.

steps Sammy Samson plastic trick King Kong drip water Joe

```
(s t e p s) t i k
 r r e l a w n i
 e w s a m m y n
 t m a s s a mk
 a r p t o o n g
 w i i n j n o
 t r r c o i o n
 t t d e k o n g
```

C **Copy out this story.**

Fill in the gaps with words you think best—only *one* word to a gap:

Joe wanted to play a _____ on Sammy Samson. He put a water _____ on the door of the classroom. Sammy _____ to the door but did not go _____. He stayed outside and said, 'Hello, Sir!' _____ a loud voice. Joe and Jim thought _____ teacher was coming. They jumped for the _____ bag. It fell on Joe's head and _____ him. Then they understood that it was _____ who had tricked them.

D Here is a short story told in a cartoon. Tell the story in your own words.

Start with:
   I remember one time I went to the
   circus. We were watching the
   clowns, when...

E   **Do *one* of these:**

(i)   Has anyone ever played a trick
on you, or have you ever played a
trick on someone else? Tell the
story of what happened.

Start with these words:
   I have a story about a trick.

(ii)   Have you ever been in trouble at
school? Perhaps you did
something bad? Perhaps it was a
mistake?
Tell the story of what happened.

Start with these words:
   I remember one day at school.

2

Na Toots!

Baby Jenny could walk, and she was looking into everything.

'Not to touch,' her Mum would say when she opened the pedal bin to look inside. 'Not to touch,' her Dad would say when she looked inside a cupboard. It was always 'NOT TO TOUCH'.

Jenny liked the hi-fi best of all. It was near the floor. It had interesting bits for small hands to touch. It had a glass door that small fingers could make dirty. When she went to play with the hi-fi, her Mum would pick her up. 'Not to touch, Jenny,' she would say.

Of course, Jenny liked to copy her Mum and Dad and try to say, 'Not to touch.' But she was only 2 years old, so her words were 'Na toots'. In no time at all, Jenny was saying 'Na toots' every time she looked at the hi-fi.

One day her Mum and Dad were looking for a gold ring. It was Mum's wedding ring and she had lost it.

They asked Jenny, 'Have you taken the gold ring, Jenny?'

The little girl just replied, 'Na toots, Mummy.'

So they looked and looked. They looked under the chairs. Jenny said 'Na toots', trying to get hold of her Mum's finger.

'But we have to look for the ring, Jenny,' replied Mum.

They looked in the pedal bin, and Jenny said, 'Na toots, Mummy.'

'But we have to find the ring, Jenny,' her Mum replied.

Mum and Dad looked in the plant pots, in the toy box, in the cot, in the beds. They looked everywhere.

ALMOST everywhere.

When they had given up looking, Jenny took her Mum's finger and led her to the hi-fi. 'NA TOOTS!' she cried. Then she put her small hand into the hi-fi and pulled out the ring.

'Well, well, well!' cried her Mum. 'All the time, Jenny knew where the ring was!'

'And we just thought she was getting in the way,' said her Dad. 'But all the time she was telling us where to find the ring!'

'Yes,' said Mum. 'In the NA TOOTS! It's her name for the hi-fi!'

A Answer these questions in sentences.

1 Copy the correct sentence:

  a Mum said, 'Not to touch,' when Jenny opened the bin.

  b Mum said, 'Not to touch,' when Jenny opened the door to go outside.

2 Jenny could not say, 'Not to touch,' What did she say?

3 What thing did Jenny like to touch most of all?

4 What did Jenny do to the glass doors of the hi-fi?

5 What *is* a hi-fi? Answer like this: A hi-fi is a...

6 What did Mum lose one day?

7 Make a list of all the places Mum and Dad looked. Write them in a sentence. Start with: 'Jenny's Mum and Dad looked under the chairs, in the...'

8 Who found the ring?

9 Where did she find it?

10 What was Jenny's name for the hi-fi?

B **Copy out this puzzle.**

Find these 8 words and put rings round them.

The first one has been done for you.

pedal bin favourite
na toots   doors
glass hi-fi ring

```
g l a f e n n y
p e d a l b i n
r f a v o n a n
n a t o o t s e
s r o u d o s j
r n r r o o a h
o i f i h r l i
o r i t n i g f
d i r e n g r y
```

C **Copy out this story.** Fill in the gaps with words you think best— only *one* word to a gap.

Jenny _____ to open the hi-fi and play with it. _____ told her not to touch. Jenny started saying '_____ toots,' like her Mum. One day, Mum _____ her ring and looked everywhere. She did not _____ when Jenny said, 'Na toots.' But Jenny _____ telling her where to find the ring. She _____ where it was. It was in the _____, which Jenny called the 'Na toots.'

D On the next page is a short story told in a cartoon. Tell the story in your own words.

Start with:
My little sister loves hiding things. Once, she...

E In the story called 'NA TOOTS', Mum lost a ring.
Tell the story of a time *you* lost something.

Start like this:
There was one time I lost...

3

The Break-in

In the empty street all the houses were dark. Outside one of the houses stood a man. He looked at his watch. It said 2.15 a.m. Then he looked up at the house. The windows were dark and there was no-one at home.

The man was going to break in.

He went to the back of the house. All the windows were shut. The small window in the kitchen was also locked.

'Shall I break the glass in the kitchen window?' he asked himself. 'No. It makes too much noise. Perhaps there is a better way,' he thought.

At the front, there was an open window—a small one. It was a bedroom window. 'If I can just get up to it, I can get my arm inside and open the big window,' he said to himself.

He wanted a ladder. He looked into the garden next door, but the ladder was missing.

He had to break the kitchen window after all.

In the garden, he found a stone about as big as his hand. He put his hanky round the stone. Then he took off his coat and held it up to the glass. 'The last thing I want is noise!' he said.

He held the stone up to the coat and hit it, not very hard. There was a 'CRACK', but the window did not break. 'Too much noise!' the man thought. He looked at the other houses. They were still in darkness. 'No-one will hear the noise,' he said. 'It is the middle of the night. People are asleep.'

He took the stone in his hand and hit the glass again. This time, there was a 'CRACK' and a 'CRASH'. Glass fell inside and hit the kitchen floor.
Suddenly, there was a voice!
'Who's there? What's going on?'
It was a policeman!
The man replied, 'It's just me! It's all right! I live here!'
The policeman said, 'Mr Martin? Is it *you*?'
'Yes. I'm breaking into my house because I lost my keys!'

A **Answer these questions in sentences.**

1 Was it night-time or day-time?
2 Was the man the only person in the street?
3 Why did he not want to break the kitchen window?
4 Was the open window at the back or the front of the house?
5 Where did he look for a ladder?
6 Which window did he break?
7 Copy out the correct sentence:
   a He broke the window with his hand.
   b He broke the window with a stone.
8 Why do you think he held his coat up to the glass?
9 How many times did he hit the window?
10 Why did he break into the house?

B **Copy out this puzzle.**

Find these 8 words and ring them. The first one has been done for you.

window Martin stone
ladder policeman
noise break kitchen

```
s p p m s w o l
n o o a t i n a
p o l t o n e d
b a i o n d h d
t r c s e e c e
l a e r e r t r
n o m a r t i n
c o a r k i k p
w i n d o w s l
```

C   Copy out this story.

Fill in the gaps with words you think best—only *one* word to a gap.

One night, a man was going to _____ into a house. He did not want _____ break a window because it would make _____ of noise. However, he had to break _____ kitchen window after all. He used a _____ from the garden. He hit the window _____ times before the glass broke. A policeman _____ to see what was going on but _____ man said he was breaking into his own house.

D   Here is a short story told in a cartoon. Tell the story in your own words.

Start with:

One day, my dad got so fed up with birds pecking...

E   Do *one* of these:

(i)   Have you ever broken something which was worth quite a lot? Perhaps it was a window? Tell the story of what happened. Don't forget to say what happened *to you.*

Start like this:
> Once, I did a really silly thing.

(ii) Have you ever been in trouble with the Police? Or have the Police ever stopped you to ask questions?
Tell the story of what happened. Don't forget to say how you felt.

Start like this:
> There was a time...

4

Spots

George and Gary had just seen a magic
show on TV. On the show, people held up
pens, hankies and things, and a man in a
blindfold said what they were. The boys
decided to try it.

'You turn round,' said George, 'while I take
my hanky out of my pocket.'

'Right,' replied his friend.

'Now tell me what colour it is,' George
said.

The reply did not take a moment. 'It's
DIRTY!'

'No!' cried George. 'Don't try to be funny.
Try again.'

This time, Gary did try. He pressed his
hands to his eyes, to see if it might help. It
didn't. 'BLUE!' he said this time. His pal
made a face and told him to try once more,
and VERY hard.

For his third try, Gary lay face down on
the grass, to see if this would help. In his
mind he tried to see George holding his
hanky. There was just darkness. Then the
dark mist went away and he *could* see

George. What was he holding? A hanky. But what colour was it?. He could not see it. Suddenly, he saw a picture of George! He was holding his hanky and looking at it. And the hanky had RED SPOTS.

'George! I know! I know!' he cried. 'It's got red spots. I could see red spots as clear as anything.'

He opened his eyes and looked. There was George. There was his hanky. It was just a white hanky. There were no red spots!

They walked away, fed up. Then George saw the rope swinging on the big tree. They raced for it. Gary got there first, and George fell on the grass.

'Ouch!' he cried. 'I've cut my hand!' It was not a bad cut but it was bleeding quite a lot. Gary jumped off the swing and came to help.

'Put your hanky round it. And you'd better go home right away,' he said.

When he got home, George's Mum slowly took off the hanky to look at the cut. As she did so, George's eyes opened wide.

'The HANKY!' he cried.

'Don't worry about the blood on the hanky,' replied his Mum.

'But Mum! Don't you see? The hanky's got red spots! Gary was right!'

He held out the hanky. It was covered in lots and lots of RED SPOTS.

A **Answer these questions in sentences.**

1 Who was George's friend?
2 How did the man on the magic show hide his eyes?
3 Which boy took a hanky out of his pocket?
4 What did George ask Gary about the hanky?
5 What was Gary's first answer?
6 What was his second answer?
7 What was his last answer?
8 When George cut his hand, what did he use to stop it bleeding?
9 Who said these words: 'The HANKY!'?
10 Gary gave three answers. Which one was the correct answer?

B **Copy out this puzzle.**

Find these 8 words and put rings round them.

The first one has been done for you.

red blood magic
George Gary hanky
spots blindfold

```
e d b l o o d b m
r u g a e h i l b
e o e m m a g i c
d l o f d n i l b
r o r e a k o l b
e c g a r y o o b
b x e s s t o p s
```

C Copy out this story.

Fill in the gaps with words you think best—only *one* word to a gap.

One day, George and Gary _____ an idea for a game. _____ hid his eyes while George took out his _____ and asked, 'What colour is this hanky?' After _____ while, Gary said, 'Red spots!', but the hanky _____ white. A few moments later George cut himself, so _____ put his white hanky round his hand. When his _____ took it off, it had red spots _____ over it. Gary had been right after all.

D Look at the cartoon on the next page. It tells a short story. Tell the story in your own words.

Start with this:
One morning last week I got up and…

E In the story called 'SPOTS', George had an accident. He fell and cut his hand.

Tell the story of an accident *you* have had.

Start with this:
> I can remember a time I had an
> accident. I was...

5

Too Old

Dot ran up the path to the house. She and her dog, Sandy, had been to the park. 'Come on, Sandy,' she said.

Sandy had been a puppy when Dot had been a baby. Now he was an old dog. He came up the path slowly. Dot lifted him up and took him into the house.

Mum and Dad were inside. 'He's getting too old for the park,' said Dot. Then she went upstairs. Sandy went into his basket and fell asleep.

Later, Dot came back down the stairs. She stopped to look in the mirror. In the room, Mum and Dad were talking. 'It's just too old, dear!' said Mum to Dad.
'It's at the end of it's life,' said Dad.
Dot turned round. They were talking about Sandy!
Mum and Dad went on. 'Look at the fur,' said Dad. 'It's had it.'
'Yes,' replied Mum. 'What shall we do?'

Dot put her ear to the door. Poor little Sandy. They were saying he was too old.

'It's a pity,' Dad said. 'Dot likes it so much.'

'Yes,' replied Mum. 'We could get her another one?'

'What about something different?' said Dad.

Dot gasped. Something different! She did not want something different! She wanted Sandy, OLD SANDY. She didn't want any cat or goldfish!

Mum said, 'Do you know...' There was a sniffing sound. 'I think there is a smell.'

What a cheek, thought Dot. Mum was sniffing Sandy! Poor little Sandy, asleep in his box!

'Yes, it smells,' said Dad. 'It's had a smell for some time.'

'I think we should get rid of it, then,' said Mum.

'I'll put it out,' said Dad.

That was it! Dot pushed the door open. 'Stop it!' she cried. 'Poor Sandy! You can't put him out! I love him! Ok he smells. What about it? He's getting old! *You'll* smell when you get old!'

Mum turned round. She was holding a coat. The coat had a fur collar. It was Dot's best coat. 'My dear,' she said. 'We're not talking about Sandy. We're talking about this old coat of yours!'

A **Answer these questions in sentences.**

1 What was the name of Dot's dog?
2 Where had Dot been with her dog?
3 Which is the correct sentence:
   a Sandy was tired because the park was very big.
   b Sandy was tired because he was getting old.
4 Why did Dot stop at the foot of the stairs?
5 Who were talking?
6 Who said these words: 'It's just too old, dear?'
7 Was it Mum or Dad who started sniffing?
8 What did Dot think they were sniffing at?
9 Where was Sandy all this time?
10 Mum and Dad were not talking about Sandy. What were they talking about?

B **Copy out the puzzle on the next page.**

Find these 8 words and put rings round them.

The first one has
been done for you.

mirror inside stairs
sniff basket Dot
Sandy smell

```
p s a n d o r a
a⟨m i r r o r⟩t
s r i n s i d e
l r s o t ms k
o l i n a i e s
t t e mi r r a
d o r mr f i b
y d n a s o f m
```

C   **Copy out this story.**
Fill in the gaps with words you think
best—only *one* word to a gap.

One day, Dot was listening to her
Mum and Dad talking. They were
_____ things like, 'It's too old,' and
'The _____ has had it.' Dot was
shocked because _____ thought they
were talking about old Sandy, _____
dog. Dot listened until her Mum and
_____ said, 'We'll get rid of it.' Then
_____ could not stand it any longer.
She _____ into the room. However, her
Mum and _____ were not talking
about Sandy at all. _____ they said,
'It's too old,' they were _____ about an
old coat of Dot's.

D   Here is a short story told in a cartoon.
Tell the story in your own words.

36

Start with:
This is a story about a girl who...

E **Do *one* of these:**

(i) Have you ever had a dog? If you have, tell the story of one time when you and your dog did something interesting or funny together.

Start with this sentence:
There was one time when my dog and I did something really interesting.

(ii) Have you ever kept a small pet? If so, tell the story of one time something interesting happened. Perhaps it went missing? Perhaps it had babies?

Start with:
Once I kept a...

6

The Space Slugs

The day the space ships came, TV sets all over the world had the same picture.

'We are your friends,' the creature said.

It was black, with no head or arms or legs. Its skin was wet.

'We are your friends,' it said. 'We have left our home because there is no food or water. We are looking for another home. Your Earth is just right for us. It has good air. It has plenty of food. There is much water.'

The creature spoke out of a hole on the top of its body. Now and again, a brown mess bubbled out of the hole.

'We will not harm you,' it went on. 'We want to be your friends. Will you let us stay on your Earth?'

Then the TV sets all over the Earth went back to normal.

People ran into the streets.

'Did you see it?' they cried.

'It was so ugly,' they said.

'It was like a slug!' they said.

'A space slug,' they called it.

'A black Space Slug.'

'I have never seen anything so ugly as the Space Slug,' some said.

'I do not want my children to be friends with such ugly creatures!'

'They are so ugly, they must mean us harm. They will try to kill us.'

One man did not agree. 'It does not matter if they are ugly,' he said. 'They can teach us many things. We must let them stay.'

But the others did not agree.

'The answer is NO!' they said.

A week passed. The Space Slug came on TV again.

'We do not know if you will say 'yes' or 'no',' it said.

'That does not matter now. We are going to go. We shall travel on until we find a better home. Thank you and goodbye.'

That day, the SPACE SLUGS left. They did not come back. The Earth people were happy again.

The Space Slugs were happy too.

One Space Slug said to another, 'They were so ugly!'

'Yes,' replied the other. 'People as ugly as that must be bad.'

'You are right. I would not want my children to make friends with such ugly creatures.'

A   **Answer these questions in sentences.**

1   Copy down the correct sentence:
    a   The Space Slug came out of his space ship and spoke to the people face to face.
    b   The Space Slug spoke to the people by appearing on TV.
2   What colour was the Space Slug?
3   What kind of head did it have?
4   What was funny about its skin?
5   The Space Slug had a kind of mouth. What was it like?
6   What did the Space Slug ask the Earth people?
7   What did the Earth people think about the Space Slugs? Start your answer like this:
    The people of Earth thought that…
8   Only one man did not agree. Why did he want the Space Slugs to stay?
9   What did the Space Slugs think of the Earth people?
10   What did the Space Slugs decide to do at the end of the week?

B   **Copy out this puzzle.**

Find these 10 words and put rings round them.

The first one has been done for you.

creature body normal
earth friends space
slugs bubbled kill
ugly

```
(c r e a t u r e)
 d f a c a g c f
 e r r b u a e r
 l i t v p r s i
 b e h s c b g e
 b o d y l g u n
 u n o r ma l d
 b l l i k c s s
```

C   **Copy out this story.**

Fill in the gaps with words you think best—only *one* word to a gap.

One day, space creatures came to Earth _____ asked if they could live here. They _____ their own world had dried up and _____ had to find another home. The people _____ Earth looked at the space creatures and _____ that they were ugly. They called them '_____ Slugs'. They said that ugly creatures had _____be evil creatures. Their answer would be '_____'. However, the slugs did not wait for _____ answer. The people of Earth _____ too ugly for them!

D Here is a short story told in a cartoon. Tell the story in your own words.

Start with:
   One day a boy was sitting in his chair listening to his radio. Suddenly...

E **Do *one* of these:**

(i) Has anyone ever been unkind to you because of:

   how you look?
   your colour or race?
   where you lived?
   how you dressed?
Tell what happened. Also say exactly how you felt.

(ii) Have your parents ever stopped you from going about with someone because of:

   his or her colour or race?
   where he or she lived?
   how he or she dressed?
   how he or she behaved?

What did you say to your parents?
Tell the story of what happened.

7

The Bet

Joe was in the classroom. He was showing off to the girls.

'I'm the strongest in the class,' he said. He picked up a chair and held it above his head. Then he did it with one hand. It made him a bit red in the face.

Then Sammy Samson walked in. Joe did not like Sammy Samson. 'Hey! Samson!' he called. 'How strong are you?'
'I don't bother about things like that,' Sammy replied.
'That's because I'm stronger than you and you know it,' Joe said.
Sammy said nothing.
'I'll bet I'm stronger than you,' said Joe.
'Betting is silly,' Sammy replied.
'You're yellow,' said Joe.

Sammy stood up. He walked round the room, looking at this and that. He lifted a chair up a little bit, with both hands. Then he pushed aside some desks to make a space.

'All right!' he said. 'I'll bet you that I can lift something that you can't. You have to hold it up for 5 seconds. And you have to do it here, in this open space.'

'You're on!' said Joe. 'Make it 25p.'

'No. The bet is £1,' Sammy said.

Now everyone was still. So was Joe. Then he turned to his pal, Jim, and said something. There was a clink of money. Joe turned to Sammy again. 'Here's my money,' he said. 'Let's see yours.'

Sammy took out a pound coin. 'We'll give it to Jane Forrest. She can hold it,' he said.

A tall girl with long hair took the money and stood back.

'Ok,' said Joe. 'What is it I've got to lift up for 5 seconds?'

Sammy smiled and said, 'It's YOU, Joe.' He stepped forward and lifted Joe up for 5 seconds. 'ONE… TWO… THREE… FOUR… FIVE!'

Joe said, 'That's easy!' And he went to pick up Sammy.

'No! That's not the bet!' said Sammy.

'What?'

'That's not the bet. You have to lift what I lifted. And that's YOU!'

'That's silly,' said Joe. 'How can I lift
MYSELF up?'

'That's the bet,' said Sammy.

Joe looked at his feet. He could not do it.
Not for 5 seconds.

Jane Forrest said, 'Well, that was the bet.
Sammy wins.' She gave him the money.

A   **Answer these questions in
sentences.**

1   What did Joe hold above his
head?

2   Why do you think he went a bit
red in the face?

3   Whose idea was it to make a bet?

4   What did Joe mean when he said
Sammy was 'yellow'?

5   How much did Joe want to bet?

6   How much did Sammy want to
bet?

7   Joe did not have enough money at
first. Who lent him some money?

8   Who held the two lots of money?

9   'What' did Sammy lift for
5 seconds?

10   Why couldn't Joe lift the same
thing?

B   **Copy out this puzzle.**

Find these 10 words and put rings round them:

The first one has been done for you.

chair   Sammy   Samson   lift   betting   seconds   strong   five   Joe   pound

```
d g n o r t s
b n s a m d l
s e u p n i i
s o t o t i f
a j c t p o t
m e e v i f o
s a m m y n r
o a j o n e g
n(c h a i r)f
```

C   **Copy out this story.**
Fill in the gaps with words you think best—only *one* word to a gap:

One day, Joe bet Sammy that he
_____ stronger than him. Sammy did
not want _____ bet at first, but Joe
called him _____. This made Sammy
angry. So he made _____ bet with Joe.
This was the bet: _____ would lift
something in the room and _____ it up
for 5 seconds. Joe had _____ do the
same. They each gave a _____ to a girl
to keep. Sammy _____ up to Joe and
lifted him for 5 _____. Joe could not
lift himself and lost the bet.

D   Here is a short story told in a cartoon.
Tell the story in your own words.

50

Supergirl

Start with these words:
My little sister is full of surprises.

E   **Do *one* of these:**

(i)   Have you ever won a prize?
Tell the story of what happened.

Start with:
It all started when...

(ii)   Have you ever taken part in a
contest? Perhaps it was a
sporting contest? Perhaps it was
a contest between you and
another person?
Tell the story of what happened.

Start with:
It all started when...

8

Trapped

The wildcat moved slowly through the wood. It was bigger than a house cat, but not as large as a zoo animal. It was hunting for food.

At the edge of the wood, a small lamb cried out for its mother. It had been put in a field by itself. Now and then it cropped grass, but it was afraid.

As the wildcat came near the edge of the trees it stopped. It sniffed the air. There was the smell of prey. The cat moved more quickly now, to where it would find the prey.

The lamb smelled danger. It could tell there was a hunter near. It cried out several times and made to run away, but it could not. It was **trapped!**

Then it saw the CAT. With a cry, it tried again to get away, but something pulled it to the ground. Pain burned in its leg.

Now the cat saw the prey and stopped. The lamb was small and white, and what a good meal it would make! It was afraid and crying, but why didn't it run? Was it sick? It did not matter. It was the prey and would soon be killed.

The prey stopped crying as the cat came closer. It stood still and waited for the end.

Then there was a loud CRY as the *hunter* fell to the ground.

The men closed in around their prey. They were the hunters and the cat was their prey.

'We got the wildcat!' cried one of the men. He shot a dart through the net into the side of the wildcat, then stayed well back until the drug had time to work.

'That's the last lamb *this* wildcat will get,' said another man. He took the rope from around the leg of the lamb and spoke to it, 'Sorry, little fellow, but we needed your help. Your leg hurts now, but it will soon be OK. You can go back to the flock.'

The wildcat did not understand what was happening. It only knew that it had to get away. But it could not! It was TRAPPED! Then darkness swept over it and its eyes closed.

A   **Answer these questions in sentences.**

    1 Which type of animal was the hunter?

    2 Does 'prey' mean '*hunter*' or '*the one being hunted*'?

3 What type of animal was the wildcat's prey?

4 How did the wildcat find out about the prey: Did it *smell* it, *hear* it, or *see* it?

5 Copy down the correct sentence:
   a The lamb smelled the cat before it saw it.
   b The lamb saw the cat before it smelled it.

6 Why could the prey not free itself?

7 Did the cat kill the prey?

8 What did the men throw over the cat to catch it?

9 Why had the men trapped the cat?

10 How did they put the cat to sleep?

B **Copy out this puzzle.**

Find these 10 words and put rings round them.

The first one has been done for you.

cat wild net
hunter smelled
trap drug danger
prey lamb

c c b c c s b
a d m d a m y
t r a p t e n
p u l n r l d
r g p p g l a
e h u n t e r
e n w i l d r

C   **Copy out this story.**
Fill in the gaps with words you think
best—only *one* word to a gap.

A wildcat had killed some _____. So
some men decided that they would
_____ it. They put a small lamb in a
field _____ itself and tied it up with a
_____. Soon the wildcat _____. The
men jumped out just _____ the right
moment and threw a _____ over the
wildcat. The lamb was _____ now,
and so were the rest of the animals.

D   On the next page is a short story told
in a cartoon. Tell the story in your
own words.

Start with:
   There is a story about a fisherman
   who could not...

E   **Do *one* of these:**
(i)   Have you ever been trapped or
      stuck? Tell the story of what
      happened. It could have been at
      the seaside, playing outside, or at
      home.

      Start your story with these
      words:
         I remember one time I...

(ii)   Have you ever had a pet that got lost or escaped? Tell the story of what happened.

        Start with these words:
           I did get a fright when I lost ... one day.

(iii)   Have you ever been lost? Tell the story of what happened.

        Start with these words:
           I will never forget the time I...

9

The Doll's House

Aunt Agatha had been rich, and now she was dead.

Her son, Robert, got most of her money, and the big house as well! Another son got a car, a Rolls. Lots of people were left money.

Grandson John did not get any money. Agatha left John her doll's house.

The will said:

TO MY DEAR GRANDSON JOHN, I LEAVE MY DOLL'S HOUSE. IT WAS WORTH A LOT TO ME!

Mabel was John's wife. 'A doll's house?' she cried. 'A DOLL'S house, for a MAN!'

'Don't be angry, dear,' said John. John looked at the doll's house. Their little girl was playing with it. It was beautiful. It was a large box, but the roof and sides came off. Inside, it was like a real house. The rooms had beds, tables, chairs and lots of other things. The kitchen had little pots and pans.

61

Best of all were the dolls, all dressed in clothes of long ago. There were lots of them.

'It was money we wanted!' said Mabel. 'We went to see her all those times! Then we got nothing!'

'We didn't visit her for her money!' said John.

'I did,' replied his wife.

'We don't need the money. We both have good jobs,' John said.

'I'm getting rid of it,' Mabel cried.

'But it was worth a lot to Aunt Agatha!' said John. 'We just can't put it out. And Amy *loves* it,' he added.

'I'll *give* it away then,' said his wife. 'If Amy wants a doll's house, she can get a new one.'

So Mabel put the doll's house into a jumble sale. Amy cried and cried. So they got her a *new* doll's house. It was not such a good one!

Three weeks later, John saw this in his paper:

DOLL'S HOUSE SOLD FOR
£10,000

John read the story. It said an art lover saw the doll's house in a jumble sale. It said it was a work of art!

'MABEL!' he cried.

A Answer these questions in sentences.

1 What did Rober get in the will?
2 What kind of car did the other brother get?
3 What did grandson John get?
4 What did Mabel want?
5 What was the best thing about the doll's house?
6 What did Mabel do with the doll's house?
7 What was different about the doll's house they got for Amy?
8 Where did John read about the doll's house?
9 Where did the art lover find the doll's house?
10 Why was the doll's house worth £10,000?

B Copy out this puzzle.

Find these 9 words and put rings round them.

The first one has been done for you.

beautiful doll's house Mabel jumble sale will grandson money

```
m a b b e m l b
n b e e a a d o
o e l a s b o y
s h o u s e l e
d m o t w l l n
n u u i n b s o
a j l f m a a m
r l m u l a r g
g u j l a r g g
```

C **Copy out this story.**
Fill in the gaps with words you think best—only *one* word to a gap.

When John and Mabel were left
something _____ Agatha's will, Mabel
was not happy. Instead _____ money,
they got a doll's house. She _____ it
was an insult to give a _____ house to
a man. She gave it _____ a jumble
sale. The doll's house was _____
beautiful, and their little girl, Amy,
cried _____ she lost it. Her Mum and
Dad _____ to buy her a new one.
Mabel _____ John cried also when
they read that _____ doll's house had
been worth £10,000.

D Here is a short story told in a cartoon.
Tell the story in your own words.

Start with:
One day the postman...

E **Do this:**
(i) Have you ever helped with a
jumble sale?
Tell the story of what happened.

Start with:
I really enjoyed myself when
I...

10

The Ghost of Millberry Manor

Ed Biggs rang the bell of Millberry Manor.
There was no answer. He rang the bell
again. Still there was no answer.

He looked around and saw a small cottage.
So he left the door of the Manor and went
across to the small cottage.

'Hello there!' he called.

An old man answered, 'Yes?'

'I'm Ed Biggs,' said Ed. 'I'm American.
I'm interested in the ghost of Millberry
Manor. Do you know if I can get into the
Manor?'

'You can't, Sir,' replied the old man.
'There's no-one there now. It's all locked up.'

'Oh dear,' said Ed Biggs. 'That's too bad.'
He held up a camera. 'And I wanted to take
a few pictures.'

The old man asked Ed in for a cup of tea.
They talked. Ed told the man about his home
in New York. He asked about the ghost of

Millberry Manor. The man said he did not know about a ghost in the Manor.

'No ghost in the Manor?' said Ed. 'They told me at the hotel that there was a ghost in Millberry Manor!'

'They're having you on, Mr Biggs,' replied the old man.

'I've lived here for a *very* long time and I've never seen any ghost in the Manor.'

'That's too bad,' said Ed.

Later, Ed was having a drink in the hotel.

'How did it go at the Manor?' asked the man from the hotel. 'Did you see your ghost?'

'No,' replied Ed. 'The Manor was shut. But I had a nice talk with the old man in the cottage. He said there was no ghost in the Manor.'

'What old man?' asked the hotel man.

'The one in the cottage. There's a nice little cottage next to the Manor. He's an old fellow. Look, he took a picture of me outside the Manor.'

The hotel man looked at the picture. 'Mr Biggs,' he said, 'the ghost of Millberry Manor is not *in* the Manor House. It's in the little cottage next to it. No-one lives there now.'

ED GULPED.

A **Answer these questions in sentences.**

1 Why did Ed Biggs go to Millberry Manor?

2 Why could he not see round the Manor?

3 How many times did he ring the bell of the Manor?

4 Copy out the correct sentence:
   a Ed Biggs went to the cottage door and shouted.
   b Ed Biggs went to the cottage door and rang the bell.
   c Ed Biggs went to the cottage door and knocked.

5 Which town in America did Ed Biggs come from?

6 Is this correct:
   The man in the cottage said no-one lived in the Manor except the ghost.

7 Did Ed go into the cottage?

8 When Ed was having a drink at the hotel, who did he speak to?

9 Who took the picture of Ed Biggs outside the Manor?

10 Who was the ghost:
   Ed Biggs?   Lord Millberry?
   The old man in the cottage?
   The man at the hotel?

B   **Copy out this puzzle.**

Find these 8 words and put rings round them:

The first one has been done for you.

Millberry   ghost
Manor   Biggs   Ed
Hotel   camera
cottage

```
a b c o t t a e c
m i l l b e r r y
a d e e f d e u g
n b q t r s m t h
o i p o u t a c i
r g o h v w c i j
m g h o s t l p k
n s e g a t t o c
```

C   **Copy out this story.**
Fill in the gaps with words you think best—only *one* word to a gap.

One day an American called Ed Biggs _____ to Millberry Manor to look around. He _____ to see the ghost, but the Manor _____ shut. Then he saw a small cottage, _____ he asked the old man about the _____ of the Manor. The old man asked _____ in for a cup of tea and _____ chat. He said there was no ghost _____ the Manor. Later, back at his hotel, _____ found out that he had been speaking _____ the ghost. It had been the old man.

D   Here is a short story told in a cartoon. Tell the story in your own words.

GHOSTS

Start with:
    One dark night, I was running
    home. Suddenly…

E   **Do *one* of these:**
    (i)   Do you know a *true* ghost story?
           Tell the story.

           Start with these words:
               I know a true ghost
               story.

    (ii)   Have you ever been really afraid
           at some time? Perhaps it was
           when you were very young?
           Perhaps there was a time when
           you were alone at night?
           Tell the story of what happened.

           Start with these words:
               I will never forget…

11

The Vertical Slide

Linda was taking her little brother, John, to the Fun House. He wanted to go on the Vertical Slide.

The Vertical Slide was the biggest slide in the Fun House. The top was 15 feet above the floor. The first 7 feet were a vertical drop. Then there was a curve. In a second you hit the mats and it was all over! And you had to have another shot.

John looked at the Vertical Slide. His mouth fell open. The top was as high as a house.

'Are you going then?' Linda asked.

'Yes,' he said. His face was white. Up the steps he went. Linda saw his little face at the top. It looked small. He was only ten. He sat over the edge.

A big lad went off at one side. Another made the drop on the other side. They came back for another shot. John did not move. He was afraid.

Linda had to help. She went up the steps and sat beside him.

A little boy of about seven came up the steps and sat beside them. 'Come on, kid,' he cried. 'Don't be afraid. It's great!' With a cry, he was off. Then he was back up the steps for another shot.

John just kept looking down. He was stuck.

'Will we go down hand in hand?' said Linda.

John shook his head.

'Sit on my lap, then,' she said.

'OK,' he replied.

He let Linda lift him on to her lap. 'Let's go, then,' she said.

'No!' John cried. 'I can't! I can't!'

Suddenly Linda cried out, 'DON'T PUSH!' They were off. In a second, it was all over. They were both on the mats at the bottom.

'Someone pushed me,' Linda said.

But John was back up the steps for another shot. Now he needed no help. He went back for shot after shot.

Going home, John kept on talking about the Vertical Slide. Then he said to Linda. 'I think it was lucky someone pushed us. After that first time, I was OK.'

His sister said, 'No-one pushed us.'

John stopped. He looked at his sister. 'Thanks,' he said, and took her hand.

A **Answer these questions in sentences.**

1 What age was John?
2 Why did he want to go to the Fun House?
3 Write out the correct sentence:
   a John's mouth fell open because the Vertical Slide was so high.
   b John's mouth fell open because it cost too much to go on the Vertical Slide.
4 Was the Vertical Slide 7 feet or 15 feet high?
5 Why did John not go down the Vertical Slide?
6 What was the *first* thing Linda did to help?
   a She took his hands.
   b She sat beside him.
   c She gave him a push.
7 What did the little boy of seven say to John?
8 When John sat on Linda's lap, did he still feel afraid?
9 Which is correct:
   a Someone pushed Linda and John off the edge.
   b Linda pushed John and herself off the edge.

10 Why do you think John was able to go down the slide by himself the second time?

B **Copy out this puzzle.**

Find these 10 words and put rings round them:

The first one has been done for you.

vertical slide edge Linda fun house John push curve afraid

```
v a v c a t f o
e n e e v r u c
t r r p e r n s
i d i a r f a e
c a h t t e u s
l j s l i d e u
i o u i c g v o
d h p n a e w h
a n c d l d o f
b a n a f j g h
```

C **Copy out this story.**
Fill in the gaps with words you think best—only *one* word to a gap.

Linda took her little brother to the _____ House. He wanted to go on the _____ Slide. However, when he got there he _____ afraid. He sat at the top of _____ slide for a long time. Linda went _____ to try and help but she could _____ stop him being afraid. So she lifted _____ on to her lap. Then she cried '_____ push!' Down they went. John was OK _____ that.

THE BIG Splash

D Here is a short story told in a cartoon. Tell the story in your own words.

Start with:
> I once saw a man in the baths who...

E Do *one* of these:

(i) John, in the story, was afraid to try something for the first time. After the first time, he was OK. Has anything like this ever happened to you? Tell the story of what happened.

Start with this sentence:
> There was one time when I had to try something for the first time.

(ii) What is the most exciting fairground ride you ever had? Tell the story of what happened and how you felt.

12

The Vandal

Two boys came out of the phonebox and ran off down the street. They had money in their hands.

'I've got to get home,' one of them said. 'I'll see you.'

'See you tomorrow, Billy,' replied the other.

Billy went home. It was late. His Mum and Dad and little sister had gone to bed. He went into the kitchen and got some crisps. Then he put on the TV and sat down.

He saw his Dad's cigarettes on top of the TV. He took one and lit it. 'It was great tonight,' he thought. First they had broken some windows in the school. They marked one or two cars. They broke some street lights. The last thing they did was break into the phonebox. 'A great night,' he thought.

He felt in his pocket for the money. There were £4 or £5 pounds. He put down the cigarette and took the money to his room.

When he came back, there was smoke. It was in the room. The chair was on FIRE!

The cigarette had fallen into it.

'Mum! Dad!' he cried. 'It's a fire! IT'S A FIRE!'

Dad was the first to come down. Mum came next.

'Get water! Quick!' shouted Dad.

Billy ran into the kitchen and came back with a pan of water.

'That's no good,' said Dad. He ran into the kitchen himself. By this time the fire was getting bigger. Smoke was everywhere. The carpet was on fire.

'Get out! Get everyone out!' cried Dad.

They all ran outside—Dad, Billy, and Mum with little Polly.

'Phone the Fire Brigade! Quick!' Dad shouted.

Billy ran. First he ran to the chip shop on the corner, but the lights were out. Then he thought of the phonebox, the one he had robbed that evening. It was only three streets away.

He ran as hard as he could. When he got there, he ran inside and grabbed the phone. 9... 9... 9 he dialled. There was nothing. There was nothing at all, not even a click or a buzz. He tried again. 9... 9... 9. There was still nothing. 'What's the matter with this?' he cried.

Then he saw it.

The phone was broken. He and his pal had broken it when they robbed the money box. He dropped the phone. There was no time to get to another one. It would be too late.

A **Answer these questions in sentences.**

1 What did the two boys take from the money box?
2 Which boy had to go home?
3 What time of day was it—morning, afternoon or night?
4 Write down the correct sentence:
   a He took one of his own cigarettes.
   b He took one of his Dad's cigarettes.
5 What did he have to eat?
6 How did the fire start?
7 How many people lived in the house?
8 Who went to the phone for the Fire Brigade?
9 Why did he not phone from the chip shop?
10 Why could he not phone from the phonebox?

B   **Copy out this puzzle.**

Find these 10 words and put rings round them.

The first one has been done for you.

crisps   brigade
cigarettes   shouted
cried   broken   fire
dialled   money
phone

```
c r i u p m e c
e r o p o d n i
p h i n d e o g
s i e e k l h a
h y e o d l p r
o b r i g a d e
u b i g r i d t
t f f i i d a t
e f i r f c b e
d h c r i s p s
```

C   **Copy out this story.**
Fill in the gaps with words you think best—only *one* word to a gap.

Billy and his pal were vandals. One _____ they robbed a phonebox. When Billy _____ home, he put his feet up to _____ the TV. He took a cigarette from _____ Dad's packet. This cigarette started a fire _____ the house. It was lucky that everyone was able to get out. Billy was told _____ get the Fire Brigade. However, he was _____ able to call the Fire Brigade. The _____ was broken. He and his pal were _____ ones who had broken it.

D On the previous page is a short story told in a cartoon.
Tell the story in your own words.

Start with:
  Once, my big brother did a silly thing.

E **Do *one* of these:**

(i) Have you ever vandalised anything or have you ever become involved in vandalism in any way?
Tell the story of what happened and how you felt.

Start with these words:
  One time I will never forget...

(ii) Have you ever started a fire that got out of control?
Tell the story of what happened.

Start with these words:
  I remember there was a time...

13

The Lucky Charm

Tommy didn't feel well.

His Mum and Dad knew he was worried. He was worried about going to the High School.

'What's wrong?' said his mum. Tommy was lying on his bed.

'I don't feel well,' he replied.

'It's the new school, isn't it?' she asked.

'Yes, Mum.'

'There's nothing to worry about, Tommy. You'll be all right.'

Tommy held his face in his hands. 'Big kids pick on you!' he cried. 'None of my pals will be in my class. I'll never be able to do the lessons and the teachers will shout at me!'

'Oh, I don't think so,' said his Mum.

Tommy's Dad had been listening. He came into the room with a small box in his hand and said, 'Perhaps you need some help!' He opened the box and took out a small brown coin. 'My *lucky charm*!'

Dad knew that Tommy believed in Luck.

'It's very old,' he said. 'My father had it, and his father before him. It goes back a very long time. It has never let me down yet!'
'WOW!' gasped Tommy. 'Is it for me?'
'Yes, it's for you. You'll need it tomorrow.'

Next day, Tommy went to the High School. It was all so new. It was all so big. Everything was different. But Tommy held the lucky charm in his hand, in his pocket, and felt OK.

When he got home he was happy, and ran to tell his Mum and Dad all about it. 'Mum! Dad! The lucky charm did the trick! Everything was OK. The teachers were all right. I still had Sammy in my class, and we've made friends with other kids. Bigger lads left us alone. We've had no lessons yet, but I think I'll do all right. And Dad, there's a football try-out on Saturday. I'm going with Sammy and the others!'
'Do you still want the lucky charm?' asked his Dad.
Tommy looked at it. 'It would be good for the football try-out,' he said. Then he gave it back to his Dad and said. 'I'll be OK.'

Dad held the lucky charm in his hand. He said, 'Do you see this lucky charm, Tommy?'
'Yes, Dad.'

'It is just an old penny. I dug it out of the garden last week.'

Tommy said, 'Isn't it a lucky charm, then?'

'No, Tommy. It isn't. Everything was all right at the High School because you had no need to worry. *You make your own luck.*'

A   **Answer these questions in sentences.**

1 *Was* Tommy ill?
2 Where was Tommy going the next day?
3 Why was he worried about it?
4 What did his Dad give him?
5 What did this thing look like?
6 What did Dad tell Tommy about the lucky charm?
7 Who was the pal Tommy *still* had in his class?
8 Did bigger boys pick on Tommy?
9 Where was Tommy going to go on Saturday?
10 Was he going to take the lucky charm with him?

B **Copy out this puzzle.**

Find these 8 words and put rings round them.

The first one has been done for you.

worried lucky charm
teacher coin penny
high try out

```
c u l l u h c w a h
p t u u l g h o i i
t e n c u i a r i g
u a n k c h a r m n
o c o n k p r i h a
y h a b y e m e i i
r e c c o e e d g b
t r y o u n p e n c
```

C **Copy out this story.**

Fill in the gaps with words you think best—only *one* word to a gap.

Tommy was worried about going to the _____ School. His Dad said he needed a _____ of help, so he gave him his _____ charm. Of course, this was just an _____ penny he had found in the garden, _____ Tommy believed in Luck. Next day everything _____ all right. His teachers were nice. He _____ had pals. None of the older kids _____ on him. He was going for a _____ try-out. Tommy had not needed a _____ charm after all.

D Here is a short story told in a cartoon. Tell the story in your own words.

Start with these words:
My big sister was very *superstitious*. One day ...

E **Do *one* of these:**
(i) Has there ever been a time when you had very *good* luck or very *bad* luck? Tell the story of what happened.

Start with these words:
Here is a true story about Luck.

(ii) What was it like the day you started your new school? Were you worried, like Tommy? Did everything work out all right? Did something interesting or nasty happen? Tell the story of what happened.

Start with these words:
Let me tell you about my first day at ... School.